TRANSPORT
AROUND THE WORLD

Motorbikes

Chris Oxlade

Heinemann
LIBRARY

www.heinemann.co.uk
Visit our website to find out more information about Heinemann Library books.

To order:
 Phone 44 (0) 1865 888066
 Send a fax to 44 (0) 1865 314091
 Visit the Heinemann Bookshop at www.heinemann.co.uk to browse our catalogue and order online.

First published in Great Britain by Heinemann Library, Halley Court, Jordan Hill, Oxford OX2 8EJ a division of Reed Educational and Professional Publishing Ltd.
Heinemann is a registered trademark of Reed Educational & Professional Publishing Ltd.

OXFORD MELBOURNE AUCKLAND
JOHANNESBURG BLANTYRE GABORONE
IBADAN PORTSMOUTH (NH) USA CHICAGO

Designed by Paul Davies and Associates
Originated by Ambassador Litho Ltd
Printed in Hong Kong/China

06 05 04 03 02 01
10 9 8 7 6 5 4 3 2 1
ISBN 0 431 10857 9 (paperback)

05 04 03 02 01
10 9 8 7 6 5 4 3 2
ISBN 0 431 10852 8 (hardback)

British Library Cataloguing in Publication Data

Oxlade, Chris
Motorbikes. – (Transport around the world)
1.Motorbikes – Juvenile literature
I.Title
629.2'275

Acknowledgements
The Publishers would like to thank the following for permission to reproduce photographs:
R D Battersby pp4, 6, 15, 17, 23; Eye Ubiquitous pp13, 20; Phil Masters p27; PA Photos p29; Pictures p25; Quadrant pp9, 11, 14, 18, 21, 22, 24, 26; Science and Society Picture Library p8; Tony Stone Images pp12, 19; Travel Ink: Tim Lynch p28; TRH Pictures: pp7, 10, 16, Gilera p5

Cover photograph reproduced with permission of Tony Stone Images

Every effort has been made to contact copyright holders of any material reproduced in this book. Any omissions will be rectified in subsequent printings if notice is given to the Publisher.

Contents

Any words appearing in the text in bold, **like this**, are explained in the glossary.

What is a motorbike?

A motorbike is a machine with an **engine** that moves along on two or three wheels. There is a seat for a rider and sometimes for a passenger too. People use them to go to work or just for fun.

The rider steers a motorbike to the left or right using the handlebars. Controls on the handlebars make it go faster or slower. The rider should always wear a crash helmet for safety.

How motorbikes work

Most motorbikes have two wheels. Each wheel has a **rubber tyre** around it. The tyres grip the road and stop the motorbike sliding sideways as it goes round corners.

A motorbike has an **engine** that makes the rear wheel turn. It is connected to the wheel with a chain. The engine needs **fuel** to make it work.

Old motorbikes

This strange machine was one of the first motorbikes. It was built in 1885 in Germany. It had a wooden frame and wooden wheels. Today's motorbikes are mostly made of metal and plastic.

Around 1900, companies began making motorbikes for people to buy. This one is called the *Silent Grey Fellow*. It was one of the first motorbikes made by the famous company Harley Davidson.

Classic motorbikes

A classic motorbike is an old motorbike that is famous because of the way it looks. This classic motorbike is the Harley Davidson 45. It was made in the 1940s.

Many people enjoy collecting classic motorbikes. They spend hours repairing, cleaning and polishing them. Collectors often display their bikes at classic motorbike shows.

Where are motorbikes used?

Most motorbikes are used on roads that have a smooth surface. In busy towns and cities, riding a motorbike is a good way of getting around quickly.

Some people enjoy riding their motorbikes over bumpy, hilly roads and tracks. They build special race tracks with steep slopes, jumps and muddy pools.

Mopeds

A moped is like a bicycle with a small **engine** attached. Mopeds are cheap to buy and easy to use. Riders often use a moped when they are first learning to ride a motorbike.

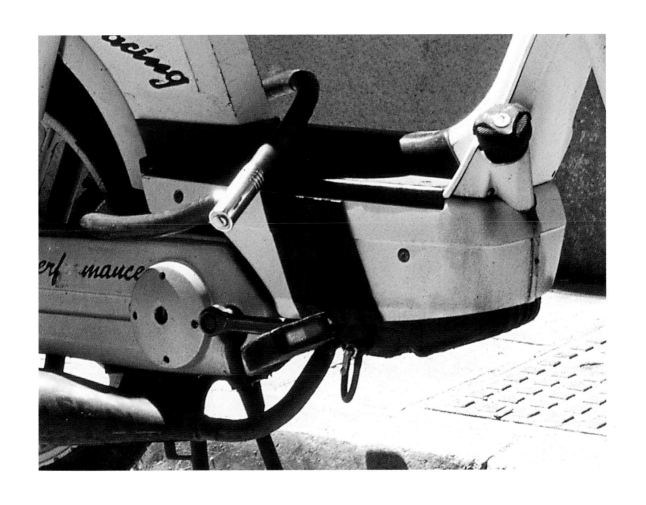

A moped has pedals like the pedals on a bicycle. The rider pedals to start the engine and to keep up speed when going up steep hills.

Scooters

A scooter is a small motorbike. It also has much smaller wheels than a normal motorbike. Many people ride scooters to get to work. In some countries teenagers ride them for fun.

A scooter has a small **engine** next to the rear wheel. It makes the rear wheel turn to make the scooter move. The rider's seat is above the engine.

Superbikes

These riders are racing against each other on very powerful motorbikes called superbikes. These bikes can whizz along at nearly 300 kilometres per hour.

Riders lean their superbikes over to help them go round corners. The bike's wide, rounded **tyres** give plenty of grip to stop it skidding. The riders wear special pads to protect their knees.

Motocross bikes

A motocross bike is used for racing over hilly, bumpy dirt tracks. The riders often slide their feet along the ground to stop falling over.

Motocross bikes have **tyres** with a chunky **tread** that grips well in the muddy ground. The wheels have strong, springy **suspension** for going over bumps and jumps.

Touring motorbikes

This monster motorbike is designed for
riders who want to go on long journeys.
It is called a touring motorbike. Its
engine is as big and powerful as the
engine of a car.

At the back of a touring motorbike is a luggage rack and luggage containers called panniers. There is also an extra seat called a pillion seat for a passenger.

Patrol bikes

Police officers use patrol bikes to get quickly to the scenes of accidents or crimes. They use large, fast, touring motorbikes, fitted with a **two-way radio**.

Police patrol bikes have flashing lights and loud **sirens**. The lights and siren warn drivers and **pedestrians** that the bike is coming so that they can move out of the way.

Sidecars

This motorbike has a sidecar with a seat for a passenger inside. Together, the motorbike and the sidecar are called a combination motorbike.

A sidecar has its own wheel, so a combination motorbike has three wheels. When it is attached to the motorbike, the motorbike rider cannot lean the bike over to go round corners.

Motorbike taxis

In some countries the streets buzz with three-wheeled motorbikes called rickshaws. Many rickshaws are used as taxis. They have seats for several passengers.

Most rickshaws are really scooters with two wheels at the back instead of one. The driver sits at the front and steers using handlebars.

Timeline

1700s The first type of bicycle is called a hobby horse. It has no pedals or brakes.

1868 Two brothers called Michaux fit a steam **engine** to a bicycle to make a simple motorbike.

1885 Two German engineers called Daimler and Maybach build one of the first motorbikes. It has a small petrol engine.

1885 The first proper car is built in Germany by Karl Benz. It has three wheels and is driven along by a petrol engine. Top speed is 13 kilometres per hour.

1907 The first TT motorbike races are held on the Isle of Man. The races are still held today. TT stands for Tourist Trophy.

1950s The first scooters are built in Italy. They become popular for teenagers to ride in the 1960s.

1968 The world's first superbike is shown at the Tokyo Motor Show. It is the Honda CB750.

Glossary

engine   a machine that powers movement using fuel

fuel   a substance that burns to make heat. Motorbikes use petrol as fuel for their engines.

pedestrian   a person walking along the side of a road or crossing a road

rubber   a soft solid material made from chemicals. It is poured into moulds to make tyres.

siren   a device that makes a loud warning noise. Emergency vehicles have sirens to warn people that they are coming.

suspension   a system of springs that let a motorbike's wheels move up and down over bumps

tread   the pattern of grooves around the outside of a tyre. The tread makes the tyres grip on wet or muddy roads.

two-way radio   radio that lets you talk and listen to someone else

tyre   a rubber ring that fits around the outside of a wheel. It has a chunky tread on the outside and is filled with air.

Index

General Interest

629.22
OXL

Titles in the *Transport Around The World* series

Hardback   0 431 10840 4

Hardback   0 431 10841 2

Hardback   0 431 10839 0

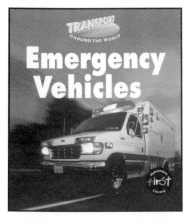

Hardback   0 431 10854 4

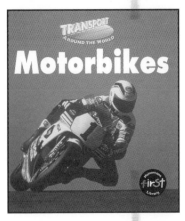

Hardback   0 431 10852 8

Hardback   0 431 10838 2

Hardback   0 431 10853 6

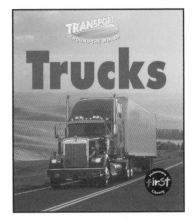

Hardback   0 431 10855 2

Find out about the other titles in this series on our website www.heinemann.co.uk/library